S0-AFM-984

ADI SORTS WITH VARIABLES

written by Caroline Karanja

illustrated by Ben Whitehouse

PICTURE WINDOW BOOKS
a capstone imprint

Meet our coding creatives!

This is Adi. Adi likes arts and crafts. She spends most of her time coloring, playing music, and making things. Whenever she sees something new, she wonders how it came to be. She likes to say, "I wonder . . ."

This is Gabi. Gabi loves to read, play outside, and take care of her dog, Charlie. She is always curious about how things work. Whenever she sees something that needs fixing, she tries to find the best way to improve it. She often says, "What if . . .?"

Adi and Gabi make a great team!

Adi needs to clean her room. There is a lot to do!
Gabi and her dog, Charlie, have come over to help.

The girls look around. What a mess! There are clothes on the bed, books on the floor, and toys everywhere.

"Where should we start?" Gabi asks.

"It would be easiest to shove everything into the closet," Adi says.

"But I don't think my mom would like that idea. We need a system."

"In my room I have bins with labels to help me sort my things," Gabi says.

"That's a great idea! Just like computer programmers have a system to keep their blocks of code organized. They use variables. Each variable is like a bin to store something in," Adi says.

"Right," Gabi agrees. "And what goes inside each variable is called a value."

"So all my things are the values—my valuable values!" Adi jokes.

Variables and Values

In coding, variables are like baskets, closets, or bins. They are containers to help programmers keep their blocks of code in places where they can easily find them. Programmers give variables names: They "declare the variable." The name describes the variable. The value is what is stored inside the variable. To put a value into a variable is to "define the variable."

Imagine you are playing a game and your score is 17. The variable is called "Score." The item *in* the variable (the value) is 17. The value can change every time you score another point.

POINTS
(VALUE)

SCORE

BIN
(VARIABLE)

"So the bookcase is like a variable in programming," Adi says.
"And books are the value for that variable."

"And the laundry basket is a variable for dirty clothes," Gabi says. "The dresser is for clean clothes. The toy bins are for toys. And the box is for art supplies."

"And don't forget my piggy bank!" Adi says. "That's the variable I need to store this birthday money from my grandma."

"Money is a very valuable value!" Gabi says.

"Let's name our variables," Adi says. "We'll name them with the kind of items that they hold."

Adi grabs a marker and some paper to make labels. When she's finished, Gabi puts each label on its variable.

The girls get to work putting each item where it belongs. Charlie helps too.

"What about dress-up clothes and costumes?" Gabi asks.

"These hooks can be my variable for those," Adi says. She makes a label and puts it above the coat hooks on her wall.

Variables in Code

Variables store blocks of code that programmers need to use again and again. A programmer may want to display the date in an application or website. She could use a variable called "date" to store that code. Each day at midnight, the value would change to the new date.

Gabi finds a coloring book and looks at the bookcase. "What if we sort the books by type?" she suggests. "Each shelf can hold a different type of book."

"In coding, those are called 'arrays,'" Adi says. "Arrays are different sections in a variable. In my bookcase, each shelf can be an array. One for story books, one for science books, and one for activity books."

BOOKS (VARIABLE)

STORY BOOKS (ARRAY)

SCIENCE BOOKS (ARRAY)

ACTIVITY BOOKS (ARRAY)

"Your dresser has arrays too,"
Gabi says. "The drawers!"

Arrays

Arrays allow values to be stored in individual parts. The bookcase is a variable that holds books. Each shelf is an array within the variable that holds a different type of value. Arrays allow programmers to know exactly where to find very specific blocks of code.

Adi looks at her toy bins. "The toys are put away, but they're all mixed together. It will be hard to find the right pieces."

"Time to make more arrays!" Gabi says.

"Easy!" Adi cheers. "Each bin can be an array. I wonder if we can do it with our eyes closed?"

Gabi and Adi empty the bins out. Then they pick up each item and sort it by feel. Blocks, train pieces, stuffed animals, and balls each go into their own bin.

Gabi and Adi look around. The room looks great! Everything is in its place. Their variables are a bookcase, a dresser, a laundry basket, toy bins, a box, a piggy bank, and even coat hooks. Each one holds a different value. And each has a special job—to keep Adi's things organized!

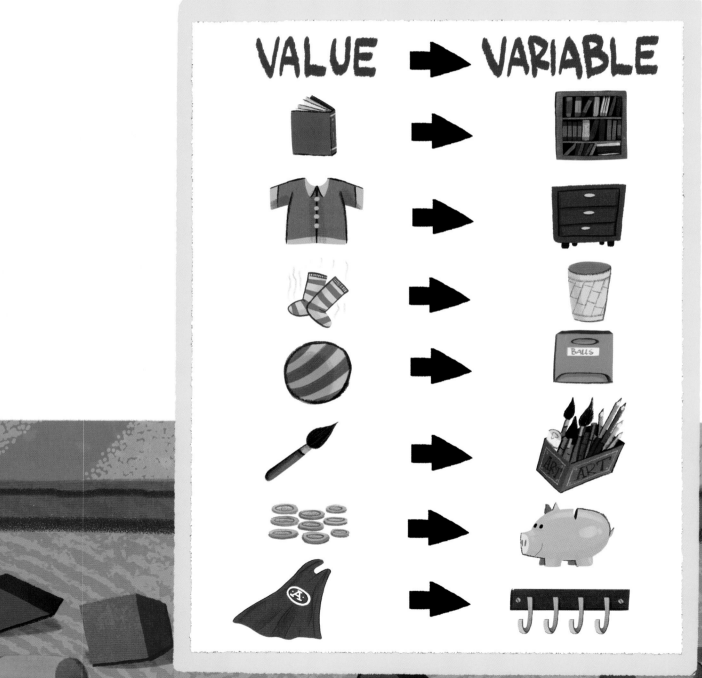

"Now that your room is clean, what should we do?" Gabi asks.

Adi smiles. "Make a mess?"

Gabi laughs. "Let's build a city!"

"I'll draw the plans, and you get the blocks!" Adi says.

Can you match these people (values) to their buildings (arrays)?

Imagine that the city Gabi and Adi are building is a variable. The value for the city would be the people who live there. Each building in the city is an array of the variable. Use your finger to match up each value with the array it belongs in.

Glossary

array—a way of storing multiple values in a variable

code—one or more rules or commands to be carried out by a computer

computer—an electronic machine that can store and work with large amounts of information

programmer—a person who writes code that can be run by a machine

value—a piece of information

variable—a way of naming and storing a value for later use by the code; a way to store values

Think in Code!

- Variables are like boxes that let us store information or items. What variables or boxes can you find around you? What values or items can you add to the variable?

- Can you sort your favorite activities by season? Each season would be the variable, and the activities would be the values you put in them. Sledding might be a value for winter. Swimming might be a value for summer. What other values can you think of for each season?

- Look around your kitchen. Do you see any variables that have arrays in them? Does your silverware drawer have dividers that make arrays?

About the Author

Caroline Karanja is a developer and designer who is on a mission to increase accessibility and sustainability through technology. She enjoys figuring out how things work and sharing this knowledge with others. She lives in Minneapolis.

This book is dedicated to Michael and Patricia for all your hard work and sacrifice —C. K.

Picture Window Books are published by Capstone,
1710 Roe Crest Drive, North Mankato, Minnesota 56003
www.mycapstone.com

Library of Congress Cataloging-in-Publication data is available on the Library of Congress website.

978-1-5158-3442-7 (paper over board)
978-1-5158-2746-7 (library hardcover)
978-1-5158-2750-4 (paperback)
978-1-5158-2754-2 (eBook PDF)

Summary: Two friends have fun using the coding concepts of variables, values, and arrays to clean and organize a bedroom.

Editor: Kristen Mohn
Designer: Kay Fraser
Design Element: Shutterstock/Arcady

Printed and bound in the United States of America.
PA021